Gods of Thunder

Tony Bradman

Illustrated by
Glen McBeth
Andrés Martínez Ricci

CONTENTS

UNIVERSITY PRESS

Dear Reader,

Long ago, people believed that thunder and lightning were created by their gods. Over time, these gods took on a life of their own in lots of funny and exciting stories.

These two myths – about Thor, the Norse god of thunder, and Vulcan, the Roman god of fire – are among my favourites.

I hope you enjoy them.

Tony Bradman

Thor and the Stolen Hammer

A myth told by the Vikings

It was **morning** in Asgard, home of the Norse gods. One of the gods was very cross.

Thor was stomping around outside the main hall, chucking thunderbolts – CRASH! BANG! BOOM! He was doing a lot of shouting and yelling, too.

'What's wrong with old Thor today?' said Freya with a wince. She was the most beautiful goddess of them all. 'He sounds like a bear with a sore head.'

'Er ... I think we're about to find out,' said Odin, greatest of the gods. He pushed his breakfast bowl to one side and gave a deep sigh. 'Here he comes ...'

4

The door flew open and Thor marched in. His face was red with anger.

'My wonderful hammer has gone!' he roared. 'Did either of you take it?'

'Well, don't look at me,' Freya said snootily. 'Who cares about your stupid hammer, anyway? I only hope you'll be quieter without it.'

'Actually, Freya, we should all care about Thor's hammer,' said Odin. He looked worried. 'Thor needs it to protect Asgard against the ice giants ...'

The gods of Asgard had been fighting the ice giants since the beginning of time. Thor was the one god the ice giants truly feared. That was because he used his hammer to crack their icy skulls.

'Ah – I hadn't thought of that,' said Freya. 'This could mean trouble ...'

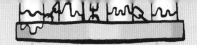

'Trouble? I like the sound of that,' said a voice. Another god popped his head round the door. He grinned cheekily. It was Loki, known as The Master of Mischief.

Odin tutted and ignored him.

'Perhaps you've just forgotten where you put it, Thor,' Odin said. 'You know what you're like. You can be very forgetful.'

'Not where my hammer is concerned,' growled Thor. 'I always leave it in the corner of my room when I go to bed at night. And it wasn't there this morning!'

'Umm, how strange ...', murmured Loki, with a puzzled look on his face. Then he smiled. 'Can I borrow your marvellous coat of feathers, dear Freya?'

'Be my guest,' said Freya, shrugging. 'Just make sure you don't get it dirty.'

Loki pulled on the magic coat of falcon feathers and flew off.

Moments later, Loki was back.

'Just as I thought,' he said. 'Thrumir, the chief of the giants, sneaked in and stole your hammer, Thor. He says he won't give it back unless Freya marries him.'

'Definitely not!' said Freya. 'I won't marry a giant! They are all so *ugly* and *common*.'

'Don't worry, you won't have to,' snarled Thor, his face grim.

He clenched his fists and his huge muscles bulged. 'Just wait till I get my hands on him!'

'But what if he's hidden your hammer?' said Loki. 'We need to find out where he's put it. Listen, I've got a much better idea. Let's give him Freya – only it will be you in disguise, Thor ...'

Thor realised what disguise they were planning.

'Oh no, I'm not getting dressed up as a ... woman!' he spluttered, horrified.

Odin and Freya grinned at each other. 'Oh yes you are!' they said, and got to work.

Thor soon stood awkwardly before them. He wore one of Freya's dresses and a blonde wig with plaits. He wore her best necklace too, and Loki held a veil, ready to cover his rugged face.

'Perfect!' said Odin. 'The colour of that dress really suits you, Thor.'

'Oh, thanks ...' said Thor, then scowled as Odin and Freya burst into laughter. 'Very funny, I don't think,' Thor grumbled. 'Can we get on with it, Loki?'

A little while later Loki and Thor arrived
at the castle of the ice giants.

Loki had already sent a message to
tell Thrumir that his lovely bride was on
her way.

'You'd better let me do the talking,
Thor,' Loki whispered as they went
through the gates. Thor nodded.

The two gods were led to the dining hall.

'Welcome, Freya!' said Thrumir. He was huge and ugly and the hall was packed full of giants just like him. 'I can't tell you how happy I am ...'

'Er ... Freya feels just the same,' said Loki. 'I see you've laid on a feast.'

'Yes, and I'd like Freya to sit beside me,' said Thrumir with a big smile.

Loki nudged Thor, and the god of thunder stomped off to do what he was told. Loki sat down too, and the feast began.

Thor liked his food. He gobbled up everything in sight.

He ate three roast chickens,

five legs of lamb,

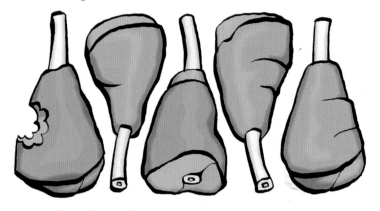

and eight salmon.

Then, he leaned back and gave a loud ...

Loki glared at Thor, but Thrumir seemed impressed. 'What a wonderful woman you are,' he said. 'Could I just, er ... lift your veil a little?'

'Not till you give us Thor's hammer,' said Loki. 'That was the deal.'

Thrumir clicked his giant fingers.
The hammer was brought out.

'Happy now?'
said Thrumir.
'Come on, Freya,
how about a kiss?'

'You must be
joking!' growled
Thor. He pulled off
his veil and grabbed
his hammer.

Thrumir stared at him with his mouth open – but soon closed it when Thor brought his hammer down on the giant's skull with a loud ... **CRACK!**

Thor did the same to every giant in the hall – **CRACK! CRACK! CRACK!**

Then he chucked some thunderbolts just for fun – **CRASH! BANG! BOOM!**

'Well, that's sorted them out,' said Loki, looking round at the smoking ruins of Thrumir's castle. 'Maybe you should dress up as a woman more often, Thor.'

'I don't think so,' said Thor. 'Poor old Freya couldn't stand the competition.' Then he roared with laughter and Loki grinned.

The two friends headed back to Asgard,
feeling very pleased with themselves. Thor
had his beloved hammer again and Loki
had outwitted the ice giants. And they both
knew they had a great story that would be
told and retold for a very long time.

Vulcan and the Fabulous Throne

A myth from Ancient Rome

It should have been a happy time on Mount Olympus, home of the gods. Juno, wife of Jupiter, the king of the gods, had just had a baby.

But Juno had taken one look at the little red-faced creature ... and screamed.

'Try to stay calm, my love,' Jupiter said. 'I know you're disappointed ...'

'Disappointed?' squealed Juno. 'That's putting it mildly. I mean, we are the most beautiful beings in the universe. So how come our baby is so ... ugly?'

'It's a puzzle, isn't it?' said Jupiter, frowning. Then he smiled. 'Still, we'll have to make the best of it, sweetheart. Er ... perhaps his looks will improve.'

'Well, I'm not waiting to find out!' said Juno. 'This baby will have to go!'

'Hold on a moment ...' said Jupiter. 'Now, don't do anything silly ...'

But before Jupiter could stop her, Juno picked up the baby and threw him high into the sky.

The baby whizzed over the woods and mountains and villages, then dropped towards the island of Sicily.

He flew through the smoke and flames belching out of Mount Etna, the island's great volcano.

Then he plunged into the sparkling blue
waters of the sea with a huge **SPLASH!**
And that's when the baby's luck changed ...

He was found on the beach by Thetis,
a sea nymph with a kind heart.

'You poor little thing!' she said. 'I'll take
you home and look after you!'

He needed quite a lot of looking after. He
was covered in black ash from Mount Etna,
and had broken a leg when he'd fallen into
the sea.

Thetis named him Vulcan.

The years went by, and Vulcan grew into a strong, sturdy boy. His broken leg healed but he was left with a slight limp. Vulcan was quiet and shy, but he loved Thetis and she loved him. They lived happily in their cave by the sea.

Then Vulcan discovered that he also loved playing with fire ...

One day the volcano rumbled and
grumbled and threw out some fiery rock.
Vulcan found it. He was fascinated by the
way it glowed and gave off heat.

'Look at this, Thetis,' he said. 'Isn't it amazing? What can I do with it?'

'Well, you could set fire to my dress if you're not more careful!' said Thetis nervously. 'Why don't you pretend that you're a blacksmith? I'll help you.'

Thetis set up a little forge for him on the beach, and Vulcan spent the rest of that day lost in a brilliant game. At least that's what Thetis thought at first. But it soon became clear that young Vulcan was taking it all very seriously.

'I've made a few bits and pieces, Thetis,'
he said shyly that afternoon.

'So I see ...' said Thetis, her eyes wide with
surprise. 'That's wonderful!'

A great heap of metal objects stood next
to Vulcan's forge – horse shoes,

wheel rims and shovels,

swords and spears
and shields.

Vulcan was a
natural blacksmith.

He loved making things for Thetis as well. One day he made her a beautiful gold necklace to wear to a party with the other sea nymphs. Everybody asked Thetis who had made it. Thetis told them, but that was a BIG mistake ...

Juno heard about the amazing necklace –
and decided she wanted one too.

'In fact, I want the person who made it to
come and live here on Mount Olympus,' she
said. 'Then he can make me lots and lots of
lovely jewellery.'

'Er ... you do realise that person is our baby, don't you, dear?' said Jupiter. 'You know, the ugly one that you didn't want to keep and threw away.'

'Is that so?' said Juno. 'Well, he can't say no to his own mother, can he?'

But Vulcan did say no. He refused point
blank to do what Juno wanted.

'Why should I?' he said to Thetis. 'She
was horrible to me when I was a baby, and
besides, I like living here with you. You're
my real mum, not her.'

'What a sweet boy you are,' said Thetis and kissed him. 'But I still think we have to do something. It's not a good idea to upset the Queen of Olympus.'

'No problem,' said Vulcan with a crafty smile. 'I've got just the thing ...'

Later that day a special delivery arrived on
Mount Olympus. It was a gift for Juno from
Vulcan. Juno gasped as she unwrapped a
fabulous golden throne studded with jewels.

'Wow, not bad!' said Juno, smiling.

But the instant she sat on it, steel bands snapped round her ankles and wrists. 'Help!' she screamed. 'I'm trapped!'

Jupiter tried to free her. All the other gods tried too, but it was no use.

'I'm sorry, my dear,' said Jupiter. 'I think you're well and truly stuck.'

'Oh no!' said Juno, and burst into tears.
'I'm sure this is a punishment for what I
did to that poor baby. You know, I've been
feeling guilty ever since ...'

'Have you really?' said Jupiter, surprised.
'Well, I did warn you. Hang on a second
though, what's this? There's some writing on
the back of the throne.'

ONE
LITTLE
WORD
WILL
FREE
YOU
AND ALL
WILL BE
FORGIVEN

Jupiter read it out. 'One little word will free you – and all will be forgiven.'

Juno looked at him, puzzled for a moment. But then she smiled, and said the magic word. 'Sorry ...'

The steel bands snapped open, and Juno was free.

Happy times returned to Mount Olympus. Vulcan came to visit his parents and they became good friends. Jupiter built a great forge for Vulcan deep in the heart of Mount Etna. And Vulcan made fiery thunderbolts for his father to throw.

But his home was always with Thetis, in their cave by the sparkling sea.